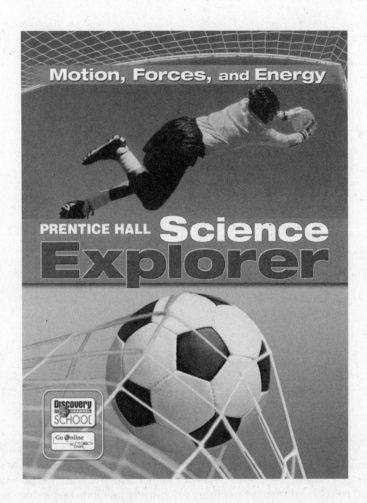

Motion, Forces, and Energy

PRENTICE HALL **Science** **Explorer**

PEARSON

Prentice Hall

Boston, Massachusetts
Upper Saddle River, New Jersey

ISBN 0-13-166552-9
8 9 10   09 08

Motion, Forces, and Energy

Describing and Measuring Motion (pages 6–15)

Describing Motion (pages 7–9)

Key Concept: **An object is in motion if it changes position relative to a reference point.**

- **Motion** means moving. To find out if an object is in motion, you must compare it to another object or place. An object is in motion if its distance from another object or place is changing.

- A **reference point** is an object or place that you can use to tell if an object is in motion. A tree, a sign, or a building make good reference points.

- Motion is measured as distance. A **meter** is a unit of length. Meters are used to measure distance.

Answer the following questions. Use your textbook and the ideas above.

1. Read each word in the box. In each sentence below, fill in the correct word or words.

   ┌───┐
   │ reference point   meter   motion   │
   └───┘

   a. A unit used to measure length is the
      _____.

   b. To see if an object is moving, you must compare
      it to a _____.

2. Is the following sentence true or false? An object is in motion if its distance from another object is changing.

   _____

Calculating Speed (pages 10–11)

Key Concept: **If you know the distance an object travels in a certain amount of time, you can calculate the speed of the object.**

- **Speed** is a rate. It tells how far something moves in a certain amount of time. For example, *1 meter per second* is a speed.

- To find speed, use the formula:

$$\text{Speed} = \frac{\text{Distance}}{\text{Time}}$$

- On a bike ride, you slow down and speed up. **Average speed** tells the total distance you rode divided by the total time it took. **Instantaneous speed** is the speed you were moving at an instant in time during the bike ride.

Answer the following questions. Use your textbook and the ideas above.

3. Read the words in the box. Use the correct words to fill in the blanks in the formula for speed.

Distance	Rate	Time

$$\text{Speed} = \frac{\textbf{a.} \rule{4cm}{0.4pt}}{\textbf{b.} \rule{4cm}{0.4pt}}$$

4. How would you find the speed of a person who walked 10 meters in 8 seconds? Circle the letter of the correct answer.

    a. Speed = 10 meters ÷ 8 seconds

    b. Speed = 8 seconds × 10 meters

    c. Speed = 8 seconds ÷ 10 meters

Motion

Describing Velocity (pages 12–13)

Key Concept: **When you know both the speed and direction of an object's motion, you know the velocity of the object.**

- **Velocity** is speed in a given direction.

- For example, the velocity of a person walking is 3 kilometers per hour, west. This tells the speed the person is walking. It also tells you the direction the person is walking.

Answer the following questions. Use your textbook and the ideas above.

5. Speed in a given direction is _____.

6. What do you need to know to describe the velocity of an object? Circle the letter of each thing you need to know.
   a. distance
   b. direction
   c. speed

7. A velocity tells speed and direction. Circle the letter of each velocity.
   a. 2 meters per second east
   b. 5 kilometers per hour
   c. 10 meters per second west

Motion

Graphing Motion (pages 14–15)

Key Concept: **You can show the motion of an object on a line graph in which you plot distance versus time.**

- Motion can be shown on a line graph. A motion graph shows time along the bottom, or *x*-axis. A motion graph shows distance along the side, or *y*-axis.

- The steepness of the line on the graph is called **slope**. A line that rises steeply shows that an object is moving quickly. A line that rises less steeply shows that an object is moving more slowly. A line that is flat shows that an object is not moving at all.

Answer the following questions. Use your textbook and the ideas above.

8. The steepness of the line on a graph is called

   _____.

9. Look at the graph. Which part of the line shows a time when the object was not moving?

   a. A

   b. B

   c. C

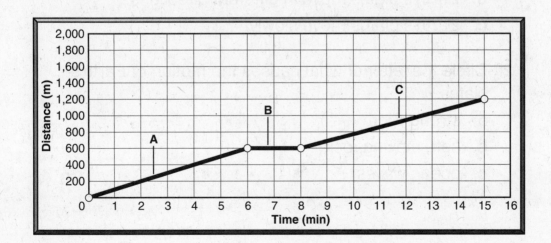

Slow Motion on Planet
Earth (pages 18–21)

Earth's Plates (pages 19–20)

Key Concept: **According to the theory of plate tectonics, Earth's landmasses have changed position over time because they are part of plates that are slowly moving.**

- Earth's outer layer is made up of pieces called **plates**. The plates fit together like pieces of a puzzle.

- The **theory of plate tectonics** says that Earth's plates move slowly. Soft rock moves under the plates. This moving rock causes the plates to move.

- Earth's plates move in different directions. Some plates push toward each other. Some plates move away from each other. Some plates slide sideways past each other.

Answer the following questions. Use your textbook and the ideas above.

1. Circle the letter of each sentence that is true about Earth's plates.
   a. Earth's plates move very quickly.
   b. Earth's plates move in different directions.
   c. Earth's plates move slowly.

2. Circle the letter of what causes the motion of Earth's plates.
   a. strong wind
   b. soft, moving rock
   c. ocean waves

3. Look at the map of Earth's plates. Circle the letter of the plate that touches the Pacific Plate.

    a. South American Plate

    b. Caribbean Plate

    c. North American Plate

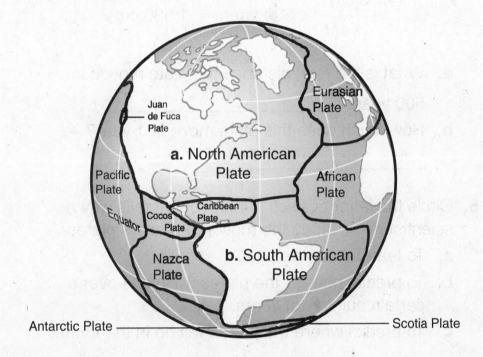

Plate Movement (page 21)

Key Concept: **Some plates move at a rate of several centimeters each year. Other plates move only a few millimeters per year.**

- Earth's plates move very slowly.

- Scientists measure the motion of Earth's plates. They can find out how Earth's surface looked in the past. They can predict what Earth's surface will look like in the future.

- To find the distance a plate moves in a certain number of years, use this formula:

$$\text{Distance} = \text{Speed} \times \text{Time}$$

Name _____ Date _____ Class _____

Motion

Answer the following questions. Use your textbook and the ideas on page 9.

4. A scientist used this formula to find the distance a plate moved:

$$\frac{3 \text{ cm}}{1 \text{ year}} \times 500 \text{ years} = 1{,}500 \text{ cm}$$

   a. What is the total distance the plate moved in

   500 years? _____

   b. How much does this plate move in 1 year?

   _____

5. Circle the letter of each sentence that tells why a scientist might study the motion of Earth's plates.

   a. To learn about the past.

   b. To predict how far the plates will move over a certain number of years.

   c. To predict where the plates will be in the future.

Motion

Acceleration (pages 22–27)

What Is Acceleration? (pages 22–23)

Key Concept: **In science, acceleration refers to increasing speed, decreasing speed, or changing direction.**

- Remember that velocity is speed and direction. **Acceleration** is the rate at which velocity changes.

- Objects accelerate when they speed up. A car that goes faster is accelerating.

- Objects accelerate when they slow down. A rolling ball that slows down is accelerating.

- Objects accelerate when they change direction. A bus that turns a corner is accelerating.

Answer the following questions. Use your textbook and the ideas above.

1. The rate at which velocity changes is

   _____.

2. Circle the letter of each example of acceleration.
   a. A ball speeds up as it rolls down a hill.
   b. A car slows down as it comes to a stop sign.
   c. A biker goes around a curved track without changing speed.

3. Is the following sentence true or false? A bus stopped at a red light is accelerating. _____

Motion

Calculating Acceleration (pages 24–25)

Key Concept: **To determine the acceleration of an object moving in a straight line, you must calculate the change in speed per unit of time.**

- You can find the acceleration of an object moving in a straight line.

- To find acceleration, you need to know three things:
  1. You need to know the starting speed.
  2. You need to know the ending speed.
  3. You need to know how long it took for the object to change speeds.

- The formula for acceleration is:

$$\text{Acceleration} = \frac{\text{Final speed} - \text{Initial speed}}{\text{Time}}$$

- The unit for acceleration is meters per second per second, or m/s^2.

Answer the following questions. Use your textbook and the ideas above.

4. Read the words in the box. Use the words to fill in the blanks in the formula for acceleration.

┌───┐
│   Final speed   Time   Distance   │
└───┘

$$\text{Acceleration} = \frac{\textbf{a.} \text{_____} - \text{Initial speed}}{\textbf{b.} \text{_____}}$$

5. Is the following sentence true or false? Acceleration is measured in meters per second per second.

_____

Motion

6. A student used this formula to find the acceleration of an object:

$$\frac{8 \text{ m/s} - 2 \text{ m/s}}{3 \text{ s}} =$$

a. What is the final speed of the object?
   _____

b. What is the initial speed of the object?
   _____

c. How long did it take the object to change
   speeds? _____

Graphing Acceleration (pages 26–27)

Key Concept: **You can use both a speed-versus-time graph and a distance-versus-time graph to analyze the motion of an accelerating object.**

- Acceleration can be shown on a line graph.

- A speed-versus-time graph shows time on the bottom, or *x*-axis. It shows speed on the side, or *y*-axis. A straight, slanted line on this kind of graph shows acceleration.

- A distance-versus-time graph shows time on the *x*-axis. It shows distance on the *y*-axis. A curved line on this kind of graph shows acceleration.

Answer the following questions. Use your textbook and the ideas above.

7. Circle the letter of the kind of graph that can be used to show acceleration.
   a. circle graph
   b. bar graph
   c. line graph

Motion

8. Fill in blanks in the table about acceleration graphs.

Acceleration Graphs	
Type of Graph	**Acceleration Is Shown as**
a. _____	straight, slanted line
b. _____	curved line

9. Use the graphs to answer the questions.

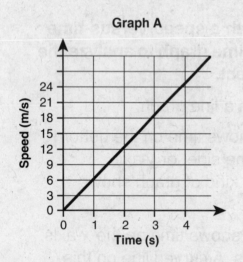

Graph A

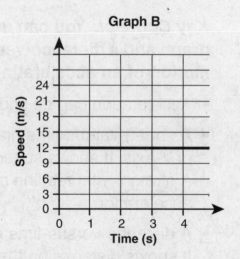

Graph B

a. Which graph shows an object that is moving at a steady speed? _____

b. Which graph shows an object with a changing speed? _____

c. Which graph shows acceleration?

_____

Forces

The Nature of Force (pages 36–39)

What Is a Force? (pages 36–37)

Key Concept: **Like velocity and acceleration, a force is described by its strength and by the direction in which it acts.**

- A **force** is a push or a pull.

- To tell about a force, you must tell how strong the force is. The SI unit for the strength of a force is the **newton**.

- To tell about a force you must also tell the direction the force is pushing or pulling.

- Arrows can be used to show forces. The point of the arrow shows the direction of the force. The length of the arrow shows how strong the force is.

Answer the following questions. Use your textbook and the ideas above.

1. Circle the letter of the arrow that shows the stronger force.

        a.   **b.**

2. Is the following sentence true or false? Forces are described by their strength and their direction.

   _____

3. The SI unit used for measuring the strength of a force is the _____.

4. Read the words in the box. Use the words to fill in the concept map about force.

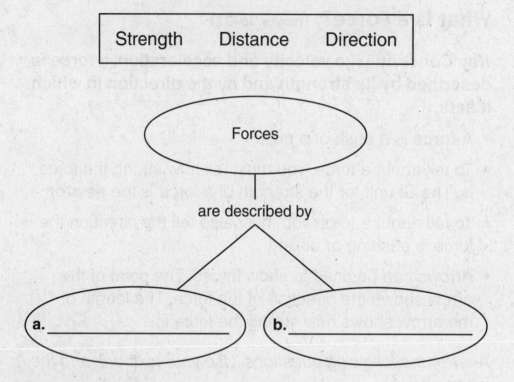

| Strength | Distance | Direction |

Forces

are described by

a. _____

b. _____

Combining Forces (pages 37–39)

Key Concept: **Unbalanced forces acting on an object result in a net force and cause a change in the object's motion. Balanced forces acting on an object do not change the object's motion.**

- Often there is more than one force acting on an object. The total of all the forces acting on an object is called the **net force**.

- Sometimes the net force on an object is 0. This means there are **balanced forces** acting on the object. The object's motion does not change.

- Sometimes the net force does not equal 0. This means there are **unbalanced forces** acting on the object. The object's motion changes.

Forces

Answer the following questions. Use your textbook and the ideas on page 16.

5. Draw a line from each term to its meaning.

Term	Meaning
net force	**a.** cause a net force of 0
balanced forces	**b.** the total of the forces acting on an object
unbalanced forces	**c.** cause an object's motion to change

6. Label the circles in the Venn diagram to show which circle describes balanced forces and which circle describes unbalanced forces.

a._____   b._____

_____   _____

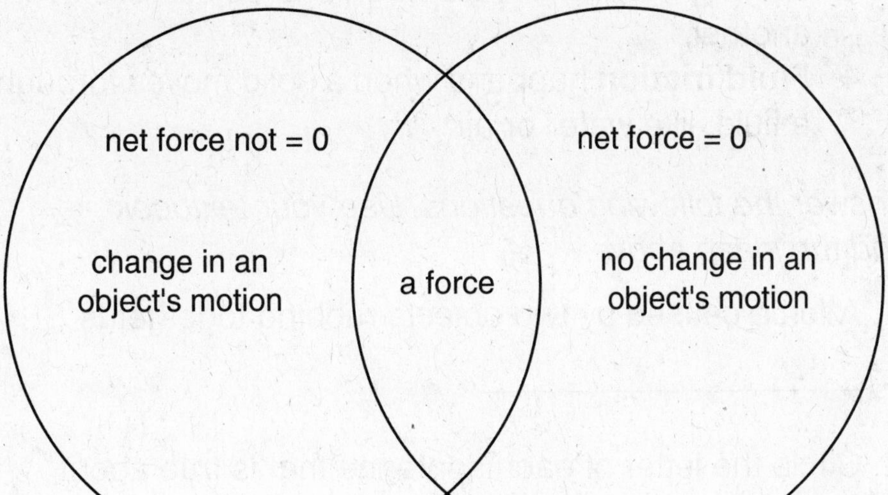

net force not = 0   net force = 0

change in an
object's motion   a force   no change in an
object's motion

Forces

Friction and Gravity (pages 42–50)

Friction (pages 43–45)

Key Concept: **The strength of the force of friction depends on two factors: how hard the surfaces push together and the types of surfaces involved.**

- **Friction** is a force caused by two objects rubbing together. Friction acts in the opposite direction of motion. Friction keeps you from slipping when you walk. Friction also makes a car's brakes work.

- The amount of friction depends on two things: how smooth the objects are and how hard they push together.

- There are four kinds of friction:
  1. **Static friction** is between two things that are not moving.
  2. **Sliding friction** happens when two objects slide past each other.
  3. **Rolling friction** occurs when one object rolls over another.
  4. **Fluid friction** happens when a solid moves through a fluid, like water or air.

Answer the following questions. Use your textbook and the ideas above.

1. A force caused by two objects rubbing together is

   _____.

2. Circle the letter of each sentence that is true about friction.
   a. Friction acts in the same direction as motion.
   b. There are four kinds of friction.
   c. The amount of friction depends only on how smooth the objects are.

Name _____ Date _____ Class _____

Forces

3. Friction acts in the opposite direction of

_____.

4. Read the words in the box. Use the words to fill in the blanks in the table about friction.

| Static friction | Fluid friction | Sliding friction |

Friction	
Kind of Friction	**Friction Occurs When…**
Rolling friction	an object rolls over a surface
a. _____	an object moves through air or water
b. _____	one object slides over another
c. _____	objects are not moving

Forces

Gravity (pages 46–47)

Key Concept: **Two factors affect the gravitational attraction between objects: mass and distance.**

- **Gravity** is a force that pulls objects toward each other.

- Gravity depends on mass. **Mass** is how much matter is in an object. Objects with a large mass have a greater force of gravity than objects with a small mass.

- Gravity depends on distance. As the distance between objects increases, the force of gravity decreases.

- **Weight** measures the force of gravity on an object. An object's weight can change if the force of gravity changes. An object's mass stays the same no matter where it is.

Answer the following questions. Use your textbook and the ideas above.

5. A force that pulls objects toward each other is

   _____.

6. Read each word in the box. In each sentence below, fill in the correct word or words.

increases	decreases	stays the same

   a. If two objects move farther apart, the force of

   gravity between them _____.

   b. An object's mass _____ if less
   gravity acts on the object.

7. What is weight? Circle the letter of the correct answer.

   a. a force that pulls objects toward each other

   b. the amount of matter in an object

   c. the force of gravity on an object

Gravity and Motion (pages 48–50)

Key Concept: **In free fall, the force of gravity is an unbalanced force that causes an object to accelerate.**

- Gravity is the force that pulls objects toward Earth.

- If gravity is the only force pulling on a falling object, the object is in **free fall**.

- Most objects move through air. Friction caused by air is called **air resistance**. Air resistance is a force that pushes upward on falling objects.

- As an object falls to Earth, its velocity increases. The greatest velocity it reaches is called its **terminal velocity**.

Answer the following question. Use your textbook and the ideas above.

8. Read the words in the box. Use the correct words to label the forces in the picture.

Gravity	Terminal velocity	Air resistance

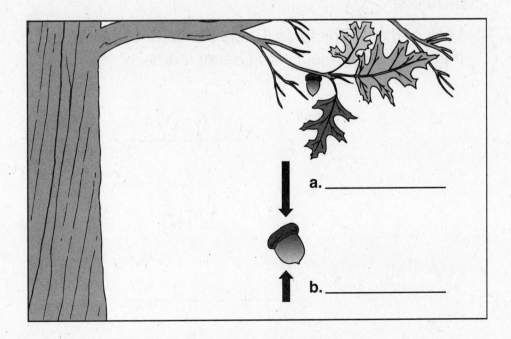

a. _____

b. _____

Newton's First and Second Laws (pages 51–54)

The First Law of Motion (pages 51–52)

Key Concept: Isaac Newton's first law of motion states that an object at rest will remain at rest, and an object moving at a constant velocity will continue moving at a constant velocity, unless it is acted upon by an unbalanced force.

- Isaac Newton studied motion in the 1600s.

- Newton's first law of motion says that a moving object will not speed up, slow down, or stop unless it is acted on by an unbalanced force. It also says that an object that is not moving will not start moving unless it is acted on by an unbalanced force.

- Objects resist a change in motion. This is called **inertia** (in UR shuh). All objects have inertia. The more mass an object has, the more inertia it has.

Answer the following questions. Use your textbook and the ideas above.

1. Look at the two pictures. Circle the letter of the picture that shows the object with greater inertia.

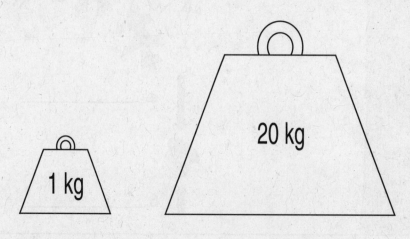

a.   b.

Forces

2. Read the words in the box. Use the correct words to fill in the blanks in the concept map about Newton's first law.

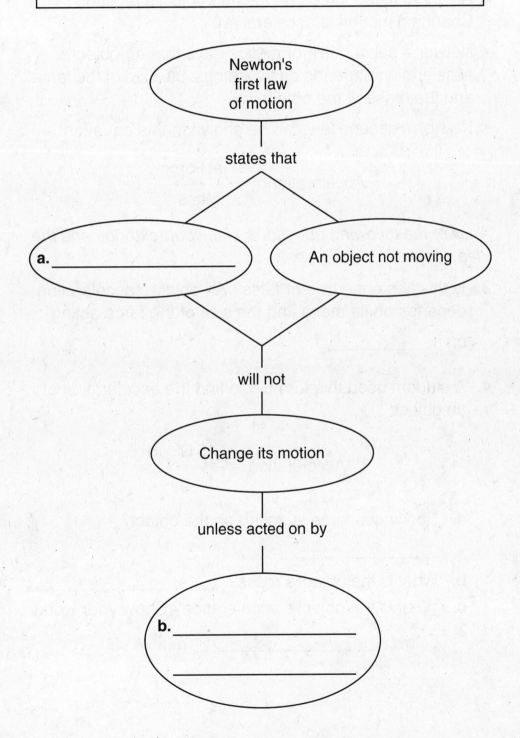

```
┌─────────────────────────────────────────────────────┐
│  A moving object      Inertia      An unbalanced force│
└─────────────────────────────────────────────────────┘
```

Newton's
first law
of motion

states that

a. _____

An object not moving

will not

Change its motion

unless acted on by

b. _____

_____

Forces

The Second Law of Motion (pages 52–54)

Key Concept: **According to Newton's second law of motion, acceleration depends on the object's mass and on the net force acting on the object.**

- An unbalanced force changes an object's motion. Changing motion is acceleration.

- Newton's second law of motion says that an object's acceleration depends on two things: the size of the force and the mass of the object.

- Newton's second law can be shown in this equation:

$$\text{Acceleration} = \frac{\text{Net Force}}{\text{Mass}}$$

Answer the following questions. Use your textbook and the ideas above.

3. Is this sentence true or false? An object's acceleration depends on its mass and the size of the force acting on it. _____

4. A student used this formula to find the acceleration of an object:

$$\text{Acceleration} = \frac{15\,\text{N}}{5\,\text{kg}}$$

   a. How much force is acting on the object?

   _____

   b. What is the object's mass? _____

   c. What is the object's acceleration? Show your work below. _____ m/s^2

Forces

Newton's Third Law (pages 55–61)

Newton's Third Law of Motion (pages 55–57)

Key Concept: Newton's third law of motion states that if one object exerts a force on another object, then the second object exerts a force of equal strength in the opposite direction on the first object.

- Newton's third law of motion says that forces come in pairs. When one object exerts a force on a second object, the second object exerts a force back on the first object. The forces are of equal strength. The forces are opposite in direction.

- These two forces are called action force and reaction force. When you jump, the action force is your legs pushing down on the ground. The reaction force is the ground pushing back on your legs.

Answer the following question. Use your textbook and the ideas above.

1. Read the words in the box. Use the words to fill in the blanks in the concept map about action and reaction forces.

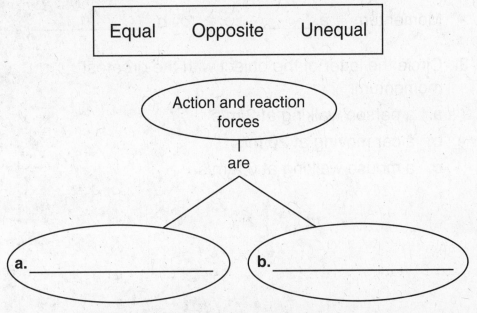

Forces

Momentum (pages 58–59)

Key Concept: **The momentum of a moving object can be determined by multiplying the object's mass and velocity.**

- The **momentum** (moh MEN tum) of a moving object is its mass times its velocity.

- Momentum has an amount and a direction. The unit for momentum is kg·m/s.

- An object with a large mass or a fast velocity has a large amount of momentum. The more momentum an object has, the harder it is to stop.

- A speeding truck has a large amount of momentum. A small car moving at the same velocity has less momentum than the truck.

Answer the following questions. Use your textbook and the ideas above.

2. Read the words in the box. Use the words to fill in the blanks in the formula for momentum.

Mass	Velocity	Acceleration

   Momentum = **a.** _____ × **b.** _____

3. Circle the letter of the object with the greatest momentum.
   - **a.** a person walking at 2 m/s
   - **b.** a car moving at 20 m/s
   - **c.** a mouse walking at 0.2 m/s

Forces

Conservation of Momentum (pages 59–61)

Key Concept: **The total momentum of any group of objects remains the same, or is conserved, unless outside forces act on the objects.**

- Moving objects sometimes bump one another. When that happens, some momentum can move from one object to another. However, the total momentum stays the same. This is the law of **conservation of momentum**.

- When one moving object hits an object that is moving at a different velocity, some momentum is passed on, or transferred.

- When a moving object hits an object that is not moving, all of the momentum is transferred to the object that was not moving.

Answer the following questions. Use your textbook and the ideas above.

4. Look at the picture. What is the total momentum of the two train cars *after* they collide? _____

Before   4 m/s ⟶   0 m/s

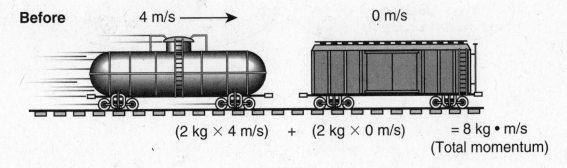

(2 kg × 4 m/s) + (2 kg × 0 m/s)   = 8 kg • m/s
                                        (Total momentum)

After   0 m/s   4 m/s ⟶

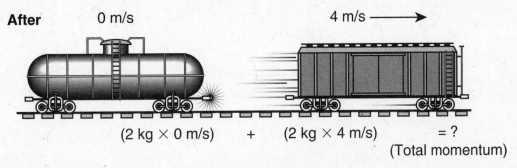

(2 kg × 0 m/s) + (2 kg × 4 m/s)   = ?
                                        (Total momentum)

5. Read the words in the box. Use the correct words to fill in the blanks in the concept map about the conservation of momentum.

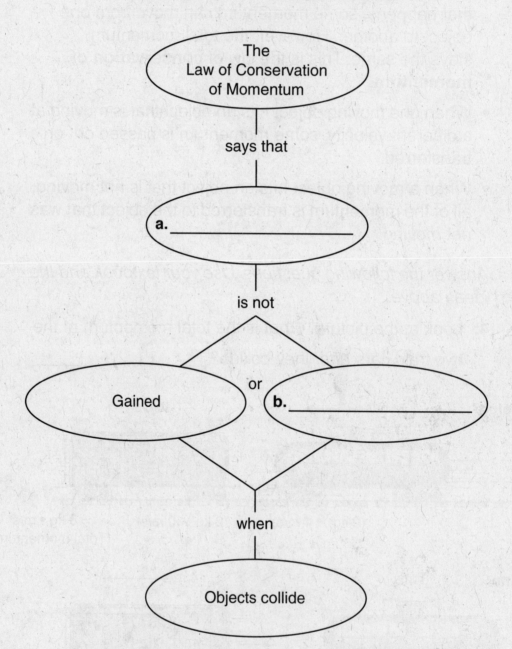

Momentum   Velocity   Lost

The
Law of Conservation
of Momentum

says that

a. _____

is not

Gained   or   b. _____

when

Objects collide

Forces

Rockets and Satellites (pages 64–67)

How Do Rockets Lift Off? (page 65)

Key Concept: **A rocket can rise into the air because the gases it expels with a downward action force exert an equal but opposite reaction force on the rocket.**

- Newton's third law of motion explains how rockets and space shuttles lift off.

- When a rocket lifts off, it burns fuel. The gases that come out of the bottom of the rocket push down on Earth. This is the action force.

- The reaction force is the gases pushing back on the rocket. The reaction force pushes upward.

Answer the following questions. Use your textbook and the ideas above.

1. Newton's _____ law of motion explains how rockets and space shuttles lift off.

2. Read each word in the box. In each sentence below, fill in one of the words.

up	down	thrust

   a. When a rocket lifts off, the action force pushes _____.

   b. When a rocket lifts off, the reaction force pushes _____.

Name _____ Date _____ Class _____

Forces

3. Read the words in the box. Use the words to label the picture of the space shuttle lifting off.

Action force   Reaction force

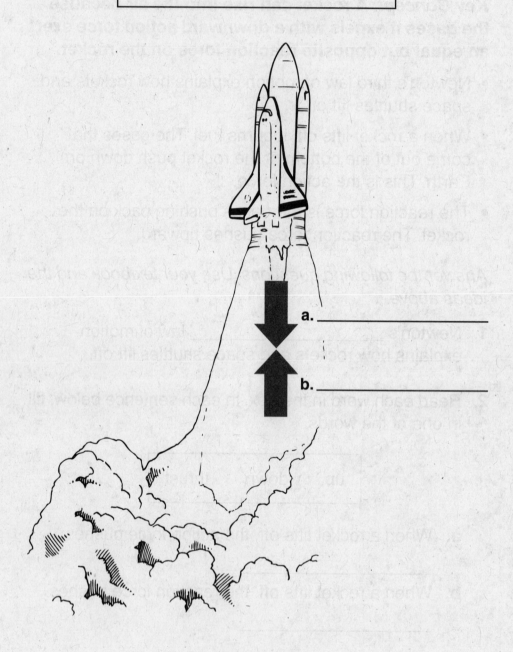

a. _____

b. _____

Forces

What Is a Satellite? (pages 65–67)

Key Concept: Satellites in orbit around Earth continuously fall toward Earth, but because Earth is curved they travel around it.

• A **satellite** orbits, or moves around, another object in space.

• Some satellites orbit Earth. These satellites are used for many things. For example, some satellites collect weather data from around the world.

• A force that keeps a satellite in orbit is **centripetal** (sen TRIP ih tul) **force**. The centripetal force pulls the satellite toward the center of the Earth.

Answer the following questions. Use your textbook and the ideas above.

4. Read the words in the box. Use the words to label the diagram.

Earth   Satellite   Centripetal force

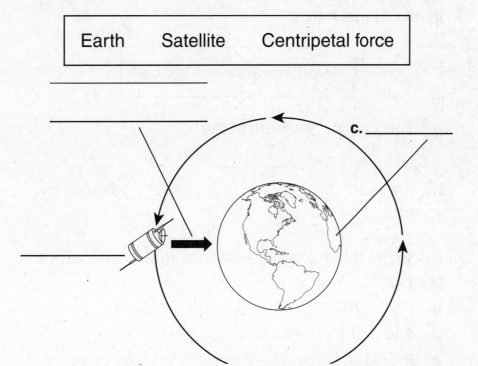

c. _____

5. The force that keeps a satellite in orbit is

_____.

Name _____ Date _____ Class _____

Pressure (pages 74–80)

What Is Pressure? (pages 74–75)

Key Concept: **Pressure decreases as the area over which a force is distributed increases.**

- **Pressure** tells how much force pushes on each part of a surface.

- The formula for pressure is:

$$\text{Pressure} = \frac{\text{Force}}{\text{Area}}$$

- The unit for pressure is the **pascal** (Pa).

Answer the following questions. Use your textbook and the ideas above.

1. Read each word in the box. In each sentence below, fill in one of the words.

force	area	pascal

   a. The unit for pressure is the

   _____.

   b. Pressure is _____ divided by area.

2. Circle the letter of each sentence that is true about pressure.
   a. Pressure cannot be measured.
   b. The unit for pressure is the pascal.
   c. Pressure tells how much force pushes on each part of a surface.

Forces in Fluids

Fluid Pressure (pages 76–77)

Key Concept: **All of the forces exerted by the individual particles in a fluid combine to make up the pressure exerted by the fluid.**

• A **fluid** is a gas, such as air, or a liquid, such as water.

• The tiny particles in a fluid move all the time. They push on everything around them. Fluid pressure is the force exerted by the particles of a fluid.

• Air is a fluid. Air pushes down on everything on Earth. Air pressure is one kind of fluid pressure.

Answer the following questions. Use your textbook and the ideas above.

3. Read each word in the box. In each sentence below, fill in one of the words.

fluid	particles	air pressure

   a. A liquid or a gas is a(an) _____.
   b. All liquids and gases are made up of

   _____.

4. The force exerted by the particles of a fluid is called

   _____.

5. Is the following sentence true or false? Air pressure is one kind of fluid pressure. _____

Name _____ Date _____ Class _____

Forces in Fluids

Variations in Fluid Pressure (pages 78–80)

Key Concept: **As your elevation increases, atmospheric pressure decreases. Water pressure increases as depth increases.**

- There are different amounts of air pressure in different places. There is less air pressure in high places, such as on a mountain top. There is more air pressure in lower places, such as in a valley.

- Water also exerts fluid pressure. The deeper you go in the water, the more water pressure pushes on you.

- Air pressure is measured with a **barometer**.

Answer the following questions. Use your textbook and the ideas above.

Use the picture to answer questions 6 and 7.

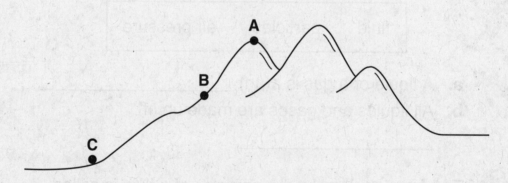

6. At which place is pressure the greatest? _____

7. At which place is there the least pressure? _____

8. Circle the letter of the tool that is used to measure air pressure.
   a. thermometer
   b. barometer
   c. graduated cylinder

Forces in Fluids

Floating and Sinking (pages 82–87)

Buoyancy (pages 83–84)

Key Concept: **The buoyant force acts in the direction opposite to the force of gravity, so it makes an object feel lighter.**

- Water and other fluids push up on objects. This upward push is called the **buoyant force**. It makes objects in fluid feel lighter.

- If an object's weight is more than the buoyant force, the object will sink. If an object's weight is equal to the buoyant force, the object will float.

- When an object is placed in a fluid, it takes up space. Some of the fluid needs to move to make room for the object. The weight of the fluid that needs to move is equal to the buoyant force.

- A big object takes up more room than a small object. So a big object is acted on by a greater buoyant force than a small object.

Answer the following questions. Use your textbook and the ideas above.

1. The upward push of a fluid on an object is called the

   _____.

2. Circle the letter of each sentence that is true about buoyant force.

   a. It pushes upward.

   b. It makes objects feel lighter.

   c. It pushes downward.

Name _____ Date _____ Class _____

Forces in Fluids

3. Read each word in the box. Use the words to fill in the blanks in the table about buoyancy.

| sinks | floats |

Buoyancy	
Object's Weight	**What the Object Does**
More than the buoyant force	a. _____
Equal to the buoyant force	b. _____

4. Circle the letter of what the buoyant force on an object is equal to.
   a. the weight of the object
   b. the weight of the fluid the object moves
   c. the weight of the air pressing on the object

Name _____ Date _____ Class _____

Forces in Fluids

Density (pages 85–87)

Key Concept: **By comparing densities, you can predict whether an object will sink or float in a fluid.**

- **Density** tells how much mass an object has for its volume. Cork does not have much mass for its volume. Cork has a low density. Lead has more mass for its volume. Lead has a greater density than cork.

- To find density, you can use the formula:

$$\text{Density} = \frac{\text{Mass}}{\text{Volume}}$$

- If an object is more dense than a fluid, the object will sink in that fluid. If an object is less dense than a fluid, the object will float on that fluid.

Answer the following questions. Use your textbook and the ideas above.

5. Circle the letter of the formula for density.
   a. Density = Mass + Volume
   b. Density = Mass × Volume
   c. Density = Mass ÷ Volume

6. Fill in the blanks in the table about density.

Density	
Object's Density	**What Object Does**
More dense than fluid	a. _____
Less dense than fluid	b. _____

© Pearson Education, Inc., publishing as Pearson Prentice Hall. All rights reserved.

Name _____ Date _____ Class _____

Forces in Fluids

7. The pictures show two objects in water. Both objects
   have the same volume. Write the letter of the correct
   sentence under each picture.

   a. Object is more dense than water.

   b. Object is less dense than water.

   c. Object has a density equal to water's density.

_____   _____

Name _____ Date _____ Class _____

Pascal's Principle (pages 90–94)

Transmitting Pressure in a Fluid
(pages 91–92)

Key Concept: **When force is applied to a confined fluid, the change in pressure is transmitted equally to all parts of the fluid.**

- A fluid pushes against its container. This is called fluid pressure. When a container of fluid is squeezed, the fluid pressure increases.

- **Pascal's principle** says that when force is applied to a fluid in a closed container, pressure increases all through the fluid.

- You can see Pascal's principle with a water balloon. When you push in on one part of the balloon, other parts of the balloon bulge out.

- A hydraulic device contains fluid. Force is applied to one part of the device. The change in fluid pressure can be used to multiply the force.

Answer the following questions. Use your textbook and the ideas above.

1. Read each word in the box. In each sentence below, fill in the correct word or words.

fluid	Pascal's principle	pressure

   a. The particles in a _____ push against their container.

   b. According to _____, pressure increases all through a fluid when a force is applied.

Forces in Fluids

2. Read the words in the box. Use the words to fill in the concept map about Pascal's principle.

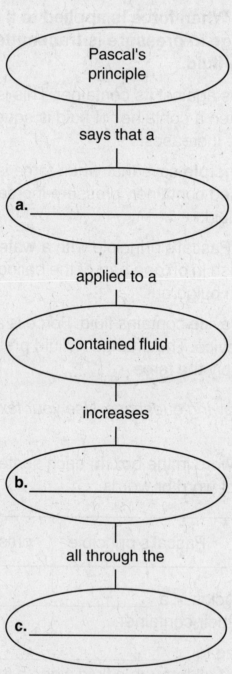

| Pressure | Force | Fluid |

Pascal's principle

says that a

a. _____

applied to a

Contained fluid

increases

b. _____

all through the

c. _____

Name _____ Date _____ Class _____

Forces in Fluids

Hydraulic Systems (pages 93–94)

Key Concept: **A hydraulic system multiplies force by applying the force to a small surface area. The increase in pressure is then transmitted to another part of the confined fluid, which pushes on a larger surface area.**

- Hydraulic systems use fluids to transmit pressure. Hydraulic systems multiply force.

- When a hydraulic system is used, a force is applied to a small area. The pressure is transmitted through the fluid. The fluid pushes on a larger area. The pressure stays the same, but the force is multiplied.

- The lifts used in car repair shops use hydraulic systems. So do the chairs at barber shops and beauty salons.

Answer the following questions. Use your textbook and the ideas above.

3. Circle the letter of each sentence that is true about hydraulic systems.
    a. Hydraulic systems multiply force.
    b. Hydraulic systems have no uses.
    c. Hydraulic systems contain a fluid.

4. Is the following sentence true or false? In a hydraulic system, pressure is transmitted through a fluid.

    _____

Forces in Fluids

Bernoulli's Principle (pages 95–99)

Pressure and Moving Fluids (page 96)

Key Concept: **Bernoulli's principle states that as the speed of a moving fluid increases, the pressure within the fluid decreases.**

- **Bernoulli's principle** says that the faster a fluid moves, the less pressure it exerts.

- Fluid moves from places with high pressure to places with low pressure. When you suck on a drinking straw, you make an area of low pressure in the straw. This causes the fluid in the cup to move up the straw.

Answer the following questions. Use your textbook and the ideas above.

1. Is the following sentence true or false? The faster a fluid moves, the more pressure it exerts. _____

2. Circle the letter of what happens when a fluid moves faster.
   a. It exerts more pressure.
   b. The pressure it exerts does not change.
   c. It exerts less pressure.

3. Fluids move from places of high pressure to places with _____ pressure.

Forces in Fluids

Applying Bernoulli's Principle (pages 97–99)

Key Concept: Bernoulli's principle helps explain how planes fly. It also helps explain why smoke rises up a chimney, how an atomizer works, and how a flying disk glides through the air.

- Airplane wings are curved so air moves faster over the top. There is less pressure on top of the wing. Fluid pressure pushes the airplane wing upward.

- **Lift** is an upward force due to different air pressure above and below an object.

- Wind moves air over a chimney. The air pressure is lower at the top of the chimney than at the bottom. Smoke moves up the chimney because of the different air pressure.

Answer the following questions. Use your textbook and the ideas above.

4. What is lift?

   a. an upward force

   b. a downward force

   c. a force that pushes to the side

5. Label the picture to show where air is moving faster and slower.

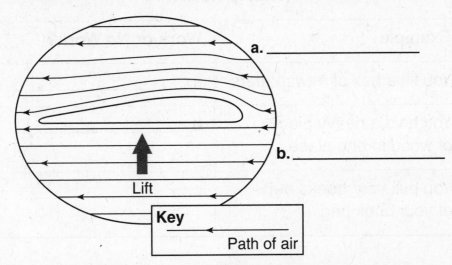

a. _____

b. _____

Lift

Key

Path of air

What Is Work? (pages 108–113)

The Meaning of Work (pages 108–109)

Key Concept: **Work is done on an object when the object moves in the same direction in which the force is exerted.**

- The word *work* has a different meaning in science than it does in everyday life. In science, **work** is when you exert a force that makes an object move in the same direction as the force.

- Work always makes an object move. If you push on a wall, the wall does not move. Even though you exert a force, there is no work done on the wall.

- The motion for work must be in the same direction as the force. If you carry books to school, the force you exert is upward. The motion of the books is toward school, so no work is done on the books.

Answer the following questions. Use your textbook and the ideas above.

1. Use the words *work* and *no work* to fill in the blanks in the table.

What Is Work?	
Example	**Work or No Work?**
You lift a box of newspapers.	a. _____
You hold a heavy piece of wood in one place.	b. _____
You pull your books out of your book bag.	c. _____

Work and Machines

2. Read each word in the box. In each sentence below, fill in one of the words.

move	force	work

   a. Work always makes an object

   _____.

   b. For work to be done, the object's motion must be in

   the same direction as the _____.

Calculating Work (pages 110–111)

Key Concept: **The amount of work done by an object can be determined by multiplying force times distance.**

- The amount of work done on an object depends on two things: the amount of force and the distance the object moves due to the force.

- Work can be calculated using the formula:

$$\text{Work} = \text{Force} \times \text{Distance}$$

- It takes more work to move a heavy object than it does to move a light object. It takes more work to move an object a long distance than it does to move the object a short distance.

- The unit used to measure work is the **joule** (J).

Answer the following questions. Use your textbook and the ideas above.

3. What unit is used to measure work?

   _____

Work and Machines

4. Fill in the blanks in the table. Use this formula to find the amount of work: Work = Force × Distance. Show your work in the space below.

Calculating Work		
Amount of Force	**Distance the Object Moves**	**How Much Work Is Done?**
2 N	3 m	6 joules
5 N	2 m	a. _____ joules
3 N	1 m	b. _____ joules

Power (pages 111–113)

Key Concept: **Power equals the amount of work done on an object in a unit of time.**

- **Power** is a rate that tells how much work is done in a certain amount of time.

- Power can be calculated using the formula:

$$Power = \frac{Work}{Time}$$

- It takes more power to do work quickly. It takes less power to do work slowly. For example, running up a flight of stairs takes more power than walking up the same stairs.

- The unit used to measure power is the watt (W).

Work and Machines

Answer the following questions. Use your textbook and the ideas on page 46.

5. Read the words in the box. Use the correct words to fill in the blanks in the formula.

Work	Time	Distance

Power = $\dfrac{\textbf{a.} \underline{\hspace{5cm}}}{\textbf{b.} \underline{\hspace{5cm}}}$

6. Circle the item in each pair that would take more power.

Which Takes More Power?		
Walking one block	OR	Biking one block
Raking leaves	OR	Using a leaf blower
Running up stairs	OR	Walking up stairs

7. Read each word in the box. In each sentence below, fill in one of the words.

watt	joule	work

a. The _____ is the unit used to measure power.

b. Power equals work divided by

_____.

Work and Machines

How Machines Do Work (pages 114–121)

What Is a Machine? (pages 115–117)

Key Concept: **A machine makes work easier by changing at least one of three factors. A machine may change the amount of force you exert, the distance over which you exert your force, or the direction in which you exert your force.**

- A **machine** makes work easier. Machines can make work easier in three ways:
    1. Machines can change the amount of force.
    2. Machines can change the distance over which a force is exerted.
    3. Machines can change the direction of a force.

- The force exerted on a machine is the **input force**. The input force times the distance is the **input work**.

- The force the machine exerts on an object is the **output force**. The output force times the distance is the **output work**.

- The input work and output work are always equal. A machine cannot change the amount of work.

Answer the following questions. Use your textbook and the ideas above.

1. Is this sentence true or false? Machines make work easier. _____

2. Circle the letter of each way machines can make work easier.
    a. by changing the direction of a force
    b. by changing the amount of force
    c. by changing the amount of work

Work and Machines

3. Read the words in the box. Use the correct words to fill
   in the blanks in the concept map about machines.

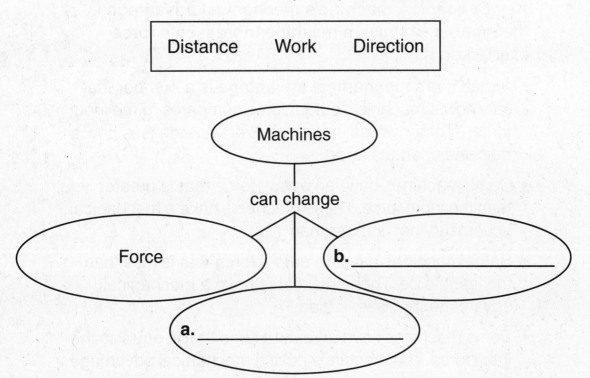

| Distance | Work | Direction |

Machines

can change

Force

b. _____

a. _____

4. Read the words in the box. Use the words to label the
   picture.

| Input force | Output force |

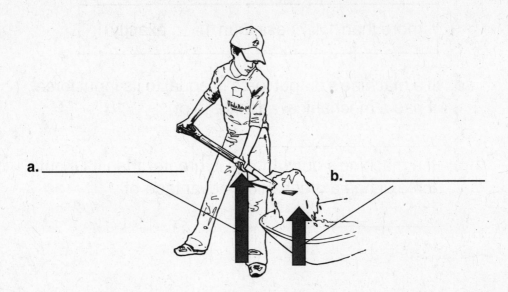

a. _____   b. _____

Work and Machines

Mechanical Advantage (pages 118–119)

Key Concept: A machine's mechanical advantage is the number of times a machine increases a force exerted on it.

- A machine's **mechanical advantage** is a number that tells how a machine's output force compares to the input force. In other words, mechanical advantage tells how a machine changes force.

- Some machines have an output force that is greater than the input force. These machines have a mechanical advantage that is more than 1.

- Some machines have an output force that is less than the input force. These machines have a mechanical advantage that is less than 1.

- Some machines have an output force that is equal to the input force. The machines have a mechanical advantage that is exactly 1.

Answer the following questions. Use your textbook and the ideas above.

5. Read each word in the box. In each sentence below, fill in one of the words.

more than 1	less than 1	exactly 1

  a. If a machine's output force is equal to its input force, it has a mechanical advantage of

  _____.

  b. If a machine's output force is greater than its input force, it has a mechanical advantage of

  _____.

Work and Machines

6. What is mechanical advantage?
    a. a number that tells how a machine changes force
    b. a number that tells the size of a machine
    c. a number that tells how fast a machine does work

Efficiency of Machines (pages 119–121)

Key Concept: **To calculate the efficiency of a machine, divide the output work by the input work and multiply the result by 100 percent.**

-   A machine's **efficiency** is a number that tells how the machine's output force compares to the input force. Efficiency is a percent.

-   Real machines always have an efficiency that is less than 100%. That is because all real machines have some friction. Some of the input work is used to overcome friction.

-   A machine with an efficiency close to 100% turns most of the input work into output work.

-   A machine with a lower efficiency turns less of the input work into output work.

Answer the following questions. Use your textbook and the ideas above.

7. A number that tells how a machine's output force compares to the input force is the machine's

    _____.

8. Which of these machines turns the most input work into output work?
    a. Machine 1: Efficiency 80%
    b. Machine 2: Efficiency 50%
    c. Machine 3: Efficiency 90%

Work and Machines

Simple Machines (pages 124–135)

Inclined Plane (page 125)

Key Concept: **You can determine the ideal mechanical advantage of an inclined plane by dividing the length of the incline by its height.**

- An inclined plane is one kind of simple machine. An **inclined plane** is a flat, sloped surface. A ramp used to load a moving truck is an example of an inclined plane.

- An inclined plane makes work easier by increasing the distance over which a force is exerted.

- The output force of an inclined plane is greater than the input force.

Answer the following questions. Use your textbook and the ideas above.

1. Circle the letter of an example of an inclined plane.
   - **a.** truck
   - **b.** ramp
   - **c.** airplane

2. Read the words in the box. Use the correct words to fill in the blanks in the concept map about inclined planes.

Simple machines	Force	Work

Inclined planes — are — **a.** _____ — that increase — **b.** _____

Work and Machines

Wedge (page 126)

Key Concept: **The ideal mechanical advantage of a wedge is determined by dividing the length of the wedge by its width.**

- A wedge is one kind of simple machine. A **wedge** is an inclined plane that can move.

- A wedge is thick at one end and thin at the other end. A knife is an example of a wedge.

- A wedge makes work easier by changing the direction and amount of a force.

- The longer and thinner a wedge is, the greater its mechanical advantage.

Answer the following questions. Use your textbook and the ideas above.

3. Is this sentence true or false? A wedge is an inclined plane that can move. _____

4. Circle the letter of the wedge with the greater mechanical advantage.

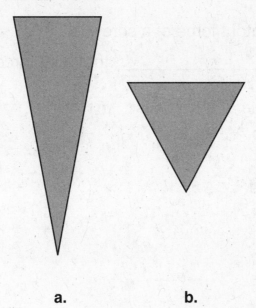

a.   b.

Name _____ Date _____ Class _____

Work and Machines

Screws (page 127)

Key Concept: **The ideal mechanical advantage of a screw is the length around the threads divided by the length of the screw.**

- A screw is one kind of simple machine. A **screw** is an inclined plane wrapped in a circle. A jar lid is an example of a screw.
- A screw makes work easier by increasing the distance over which a force is exerted.
- A screw's output force is greater than the input force.

Answer the following questions. Use your textbook and the ideas above.

5. An inclined plane wrapped in a circle is a(an)

   _____.

6. Read each word in the box. In the sentence below, fill in the correct words.

greater than	less than	equal to

   a. The output force of a screw is

      _____ the input force.

7. An example of a screw is
   a. a ramp.
   b. a knife.
   c. a jar lid.

Work and Machines

Levers (pages 128–129)

Key Concept: **The ideal mechanical advantage of a lever is determined by dividing the distance from the fulcrum to the input force by the distance from the fulcrum to the output force.**

- A lever is one kind of simple machine. A **lever** is a bar that moves around a fixed point called a **fulcrum**. There are three kinds, or classes, of levers.

- In a first-class lever, the fulcrum is between the input force and output force. First-class levers change the direction of a force. A seesaw is a first-class lever.

- In a second-class lever, the output force is between the fulcrum and the input force. Second-class levers increase a force. A wheelbarrow is a second-class lever.

- In a third-class lever, the input force is between the fulcrum and the output force. Third-class levers increase the distance over which a force is exerted. A hockey stick is a third-class lever.

Answer the following questions. Use your textbook and the ideas above.

8. Draw a line from each term to its meaning.

Term	Meaning
fulcrum	**a.** a bar that moves
	b. a fixed point
lever	

9. Circle the letter of each example of a lever.
   - **a.** hockey stick
   - **b.** screw
   - **c.** wheelbarrow

Work and Machines

10. Read the words in the box. Use the correct words to label the diagram.

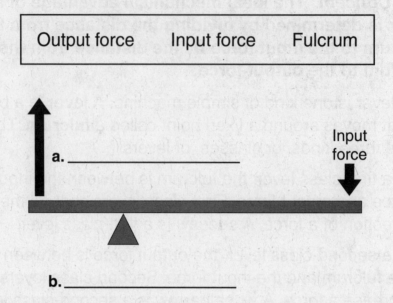

| Output force   Input force   Fulcrum |

a. _____

Input force

b. _____

Wheel and Axle (pages 130–132)

Key Concept: **You can find the mechanical advantage of a wheel and axle by dividing the radius of the wheel by the radius of the axle.**

- A wheel and axle is one kind of simple machine. A **wheel and axle** is two circular objects that are joined together. A screwdriver and a doorknob are examples of wheel and axles.

- Some wheel and axles increase force. Other wheel and axles increase the distance over which a force is exerted.

Answer the following questions. Use your textbook and the ideas above.

11. Circle the letter of each example of a wheel and axle.

    a. doorknob

    b. screwdriver

    c. screw

12. Circle each way a wheel and axle can help you do work.

   a. reduce the work

   b. increase the force

   c. increase the distance over which a force is exerted

Pulley (pages 132–133)

Key Concept: **The ideal mechanical advantage of a pulley is equal to the number of sections of rope that support the object.**

- A pulley is one kind of simple machine. A **pulley** is a wheel with a rope or cable wrapped around it. A pulley is used to raise a flag on a flagpole.

- Pulleys can change the amount or direction of the input force.

Answer the following questions. Use your textbook and the ideas above.

13. Is this sentence true or false? A pulley changes the amount of work needed to raise a flag. _____

14. You can use a(an) _____ to raise a flag up a flagpole.

Simple Machines in the Body (page 134)

Key Concept: **Most of the machines in your body are levers that consist of bones and muscles.**

- Levers are found in your body. Your arm works as a lever when you bend your elbow. Your foot acts as a lever when you take a step.

- Wedges are found in your body, too. Your front teeth are wedges that help you bite through food.

Work and Machines

Answer the following questions. Use your textbook and the ideas on page 57.

15. When you bend your knee, your leg acts as a

    a. wedge.

    b. lever.

    c. pulley.

16. When you bite into an apple, your front teeth act as

    a. wedges.

    b. levers.

    c. pulleys.

Compound Machines (page 135)

Key Concept: **The ideal mechanical advantage of a compound machine is the product of the individual ideal mechanical advantages of the simple machines that make it up.**

- A **compound machine** is made of two or more simple machines.

- Most machines you use are compound machines. A bicycle is one example of a compound machine.

Answer the following questions. Use your textbook and the ideas above.

17. A machine that is made of two or more simple machines is called a(an) _____.

18. Is the following sentence true or false? A bicycle is an example of a simple machine. _____

Energy

What Is Energy? (pages 146–150)

Energy, Work, and Power (page 147)

Key Concept: If the transfer of energy is work, then power is the rate at which energy is transferred, or the amount of energy transferred in a unit of time.

- When a force moves an object, work is done. **Energy** is the ability to do work.

- When work is done on an object, some energy transfers to that object.

- Power tells how much energy is transferred in each unit of time. The formula for power is:

$$\text{Power} = \frac{\text{Energy transferred}}{\text{Time}}$$

Answer the following questions. Use your textbook and the ideas above.

1. Draw a line from each term to its meaning.

Term	Meaning
work	**a.** amount of energy transferred in each unit of time
energy	
power	**b.** the ability to do work
	c. when a force causes motion

2. Is the following sentence true or false? Force is the ability to do work. _____

Name _____ Date _____ Class _____

Energy

Kinetic Energy (pages 147–148)

Key Concept: Two basic kinds of energy are kinetic energy and potential energy.

- **Kinetic energy** is energy of motion.

- The amount of kinetic energy an object has depends on its mass and its velocity.

- The faster an object moves, the more kinetic energy it has. The more mass an object has, the more kinetic energy it has.

Answer the following questions. Use your textbook and the ideas above.

3. The energy of motion is called

   _____.

4. Read the words in the box. Use the words to fill in the blanks in the concept map about kinetic energy.

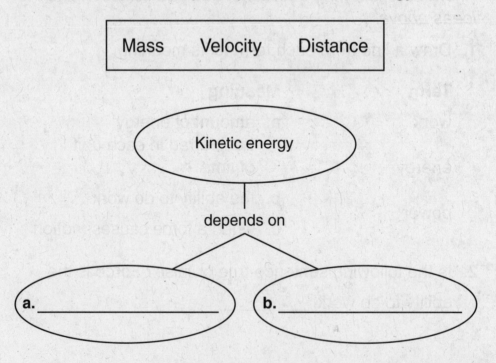

Mass   Velocity   Distance

Kinetic energy

depends on

a. _____   b. _____

Energy

Potential Energy (pages 149–150)

Key Concept: **Two basic kinds of energy are kinetic energy and potential energy.**

- **Potential energy** is stored energy. Energy can be stored in an object because of where it is or because of its shape.

- A book sitting on a desk has potential energy. Energy was stored in the book when it was lifted onto the desk. Potential energy due to an object's height is called **gravitational potential energy**. The greater an object's height, the more gravitational potential energy it has. The greater an object's weight, the more gravitational potential energy it has.

- **Elastic potential energy** is the energy in springs and archery bows.

Answer the following questions. Use your textbook and the ideas above.

5. Stored energy is called _____.

6. Read each word in the box. In each sentence below, fill in the correct word or words.

gravitational potential   kinetic
elastic potential

    a. A stretched rubber band has

    _____ energy.

    b. A book on top of a desk has

    _____ energy.

Energy

Use the pictures to answer questions 7 and 8.

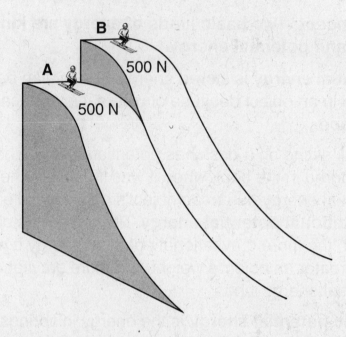

7. Both skiers above weigh 500 N. Which skier, A or B, has more gravitational potential energy? _____

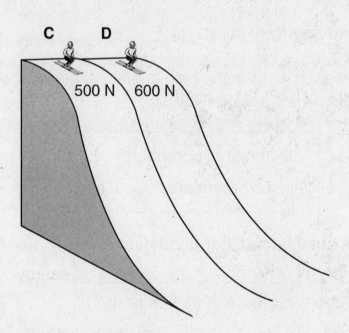

8. Skier C above weighs 500 N. Skier D weighs 600 N. Which skier, C or D, has more gravitational potential energy? _____

Forms of Energy (pages 151–155)

Mechanical Energy (pages 151–152)

Key Concept: **You can find an object's mechanical energy by adding the object's kinetic energy and potential energy.**

- **Mechanical energy** is the energy an object has because of its position and its motion.

- You can find an object's mechanical energy by adding its kinetic energy and its potential energy. Use this formula:

$$\text{Mechanical energy} = \text{Potential energy} + \text{Kinetic energy}$$

Answer the following questions. Use your textbook and the ideas above.

1. Read the words in the box. Use the words to fill in the blanks in the concept map about mechanical energy.

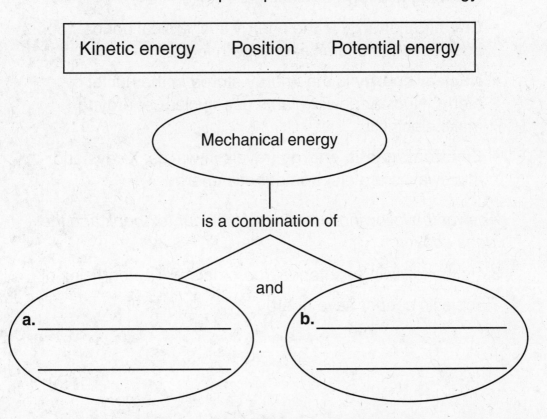

| Kinetic energy | Position | Potential energy |

Mechanical energy

is a combination of

a. _____

and

b. _____

2. Circle the letter of the formula for mechanical energy.

a. Mechanical energy = Potential energy − Kinetic energy

b. Mechanical energy = Potential energy + Kinetic energy

c. Mechanical energy = Potential energy × Kinetic energy

Other Forms of Energy (pages 153–155)

Key Concept: **Forms of energy associated with the particles of objects include thermal energy, electrical energy, chemical energy, nuclear energy, and electromagnetic energy.**

- **Thermal energy** is the total energy in the particles of an object. Hot things have more thermal energy than cold things.

- **Electrical energy** is the energy of electrical charges. Lightning is a form of electrical energy.

- **Chemical energy** is the energy in chemical bonds. Your body uses the chemical energy in food.

- **Nuclear energy** is the energy stored in the nuclei of atoms. Nuclear power plants use nuclear energy to make electricity.

- **Electromagnetic energy** travels in waves. X-rays and microwaves are electromagnetic energy.

Answer the following questions. Use your textbook and the ideas above.

3. Is the following sentence true or false? The particles of objects cannot have energy. _____

Energy

4. Read the words in the box. Use the words to fill in the blanks in the table about forms of energy.

Thermal energy	Chemical energy
Nuclear energy	Electromagnetic energy
Electrical energy	

Type of Energy	Description
Thermal energy	total energy of the particles in an object
a. _____	energy stored in the nuclei of atoms
b. _____	energy in chemical bonds
c. _____	travels in waves
d. _____	energy of electrical changes

Energy

Energy Transformations and Conservation (pages 158–163)

Energy Transformations (pages 158–159)

Key Concept: **Most forms of energy can be transformed into other forms.**

- Energy can change forms. An **energy transformation** is a change from one form of energy to another form of energy.

- Energy transformations happen all around you. A toaster changes electrical energy to thermal energy. Your body changes the chemical energy in food to mechanical energy as you move.

- Sometimes energy changes forms once to do work. These are single transformations.

- Sometimes energy changes forms several times to do work. These are multiple transformations.

Answer the following questions. Use your textbook and the ideas above.

1. Is this sentence true or false? Energy never changes forms. _____

2. In each sentence below, fill in the correct word.
   a. When a toaster changes electrical energy to thermal energy, it is a(an) _____ transformation.
   b. A car's engine changes the form of energy several times. This is a(an) _____ transformation.

Energy

Transformations Between Potential and Kinetic Energy (pages 160–161)

Key Concept: **One of the most common energy transformations is the transformation between potential energy and kinetic energy.**

- Kinetic energy is the energy of motion. Potential energy is stored energy. Energy can change from potential to kinetic and back again.

- Energy changes form when an object moves up or down. The object has the most potential energy at its highest point. The object has the most kinetic energy at its lowest point.

- A pendulum changes energy as it swings. It has the most potential energy at its highest point. It has the most kinetic energy at its lowest point.

Answer the following questions. Use your textbook and the ideas above.

Use the picture to answer questions 3 and 4.

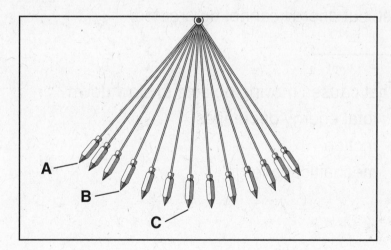

3. At what point does the pendulum have the greatest potential energy? _____

4. At what point does the pendulum have the greatest kinetic energy? _____

Energy

Conservation of Energy (pages 162–163)

Key Concept: **According to the law of conservation of energy, energy cannot be created or destroyed.**

- The amount of energy does not change when energy changes forms. Energy is not lost. Energy is not created. This is the **law of conservation of energy**.

- Energy is not lost when a moving object slows down. Friction changes mechanical energy to thermal energy.

- For example, a spinning top slows down because of friction. Friction with the floor and friction with the air changes some of the top's mechanical energy to thermal energy.

- Energy can be created if matter is destroyed. **Matter** is anything that has mass. A tiny bit of matter can make a huge amount of energy.

Answer the following questions. Use your textbook and the ideas above.

5. Is the following sentence true or false? Energy can be lost, but energy cannot be created.

   _____

6. What causes moving objects to slow down?
   a. total energy decreases
   b. friction
   c. mechanical energy

Energy

7. Read the words in the box. Use the words to fill in the blanks in the concept map about the conservation of energy.

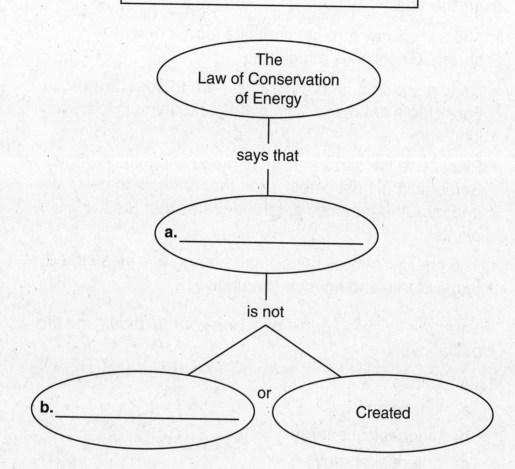

Energy   Lost   Transformed

The
Law of Conservation
of Energy

says that

a. _____

is not

b. _____   or   Created

Energy

Energy and Fossil Fuels (pages 166–169)

Formation of Fossil Fuels (pages 166–168)

Key Concept: **Fossil fuels contain energy that came from the sun.**

- A fuel is something that contains stored potential energy. Gasoline is a fuel.

- Coal, petroleum, and natural gas are all **fossil fuels**. Fossil fuels are made from plants and animals that lived long ago.

- Plants use the sun's energy to make chemical energy. Some animals eat plants and other animals to get energy. Other animals eat the animals that ate the plants.

- The energy in fossil fuels is the energy that was stored in the plants and animals long ago.

Answer the following questions. Use your textbook and the ideas above.

1. A fuel has
   a. kinetic energy.
   b. mechanical energy.
   c. potential energy.

2. Where did the energy in fossil fuels originally come from?
   a. the sun
   b. animals
   c. fossils

Energy

3. Read each word in the box. In each sentence below, fill in the correct word or words.

| fossil fuels   potential energy   sunlight |

   a. The energy in a fuel is _____.

   b. The energy in _____ is the energy from plants and animals long ago.

4. Circle the letter of each fossil fuel.

   a. wood

   b. natural gas

   c. coal

Use of Fossil Fuels (pages 168–169)

***Key Concept:* Fossil fuels can be burned to release the chemical energy stored millions of years ago.**

- **Combustion** means burning. During combustion, chemical energy is changed to thermal energy.

- A fossil fuel is burned at a power plant. The chemical energy in the fossil fuel is changed to thermal energy. The thermal energy heats water to make steam. The steam turns a turbine. The turbine changes thermal energy to mechanical energy. A generator changes mechanical energy to electrical energy. The electrical energy is used in homes and businesses to do work.

Answer the following questions. Use your textbook and the ideas above.

5. Chemical energy is changed to thermal energy during

_____.

Energy

6. Read the words in the box. Use the correct words to fill in the blanks in the flowchart about energy transformations at a power plant.

```
┌─────────────────────────────────────────────────┐
│  thermal energy       electrical energy           │
│  mechanical energy                                │
└─────────────────────────────────────────────────┘
```

```
┌─────────────────────────────────────────────────┐
│        Fossil fuels are burned at a power plant.  │
└─────────────────────────────────────────────────┘
                        ↓
┌─────────────────────────────────────────────────┐
│  Chemical energy is changed to  a._____ │
│                                                   │
│              _____ .             │
└─────────────────────────────────────────────────┘
                        ↓
┌─────────────────────────────────────────────────┐
│    Thermal energy is used to heat water and make steam. │
└─────────────────────────────────────────────────┘
                        ↓
┌─────────────────────────────────────────────────┐
│  Steam turns a turbine, which changes thermal energy to │
│                                                   │
│        b. _____ .               │
└─────────────────────────────────────────────────┘
                        ↓
┌─────────────────────────────────────────────────┐
│      A generator changes mechanical energy to     │
│                                                   │
│        c. _____ .               │
└─────────────────────────────────────────────────┘
```

Thermal Energy and Heat

Temperature, Thermal Energy, and Heat (pages 176–181)

Temperature (pages 176–178)

Key Concept: **The three common scales for measuring temperature are the Fahrenheit, Celsius, and Kelvin scales.**

- All objects are made up of tiny particles. **Temperature** tells how quickly the particles in an object are moving.

- The particles in a warm object move quickly. The object has a high temperature. The particles in a cool object move slowly. The object has a low temperature.

- A thermometer measures temperature. A thermometer contains liquid. The level of the liquid tells the temperature.

- There are three temperature scales that are commonly used. On the **Fahrenheit scale**, water freezes at 32°F and boils at 212°F. On the **Celsius scale**, water freezes at 0°C and boils at 100°C. On the **Kelvin scale**, water freezes at 273 K and boils at 373 K.

Answer the following questions. Use your textbook and the ideas above.

1. A measure of how quickly the particles in an object are moving is _____.

2. Which of these has the fastest-moving particles?
   a. an ice cube
   b. a cup of cold water
   c. a mug of boiling water

Thermal Energy and Heat

3. A tool used to measure temperature is an(an)

_____.

4. Read the words in the box. Use the words to fill in the blanks in the table about temperature scales.

Fahrenheit   Celsius   Kelvin

Temperature		
Scale	**Water Freezes**	**Water Boils**
a. _____	273	373
b. _____	0°C	100°C
c. _____	32°F	212°F

5. Is the following sentence true or false? The particles in a cool object move more quickly than the particles

in a warm object. _____

Thermal Energy and Heat (pages 178–179)

Key Concept: **Heat is thermal energy moving from a warmer object to a cooler object.**

- Thermal energy is the total energy of all the particles in an object.

- Thermal energy depends on how fast the particles are moving. Thermal energy also depends on how many particles there are. That is why a liter of hot water has more thermal energy than a drop of water at the same temperature.

- **Heat** is moving thermal energy. Heat always moves from a warmer object to a cooler object.

Answer the following questions. Use your textbook and the ideas above.

6. Circle the letters of two things that determine how much thermal energy an object has.
   a. how many particles it has
   b. which temperature scale is used
   c. how fast its particles are moving

7. Thermal energy that moves from a warmer object to a cooler object is called _____.

8. Draw arrows in the picture to show in which direction heat moves.

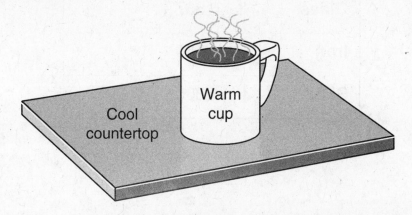

Thermal Energy and Heat

Specific Heat (pages 180–181)

Key Concept: **A material with a high specific heat can absorb a great deal of thermal energy without a great change in temperature.**

• When an object is heated, its temperature rises. How much its temperature rises depends on its specific heat.

• **Specific heat** is the amount of energy needed to raise the temperature of 1 kilogram of a material by 1 kelvin.

• Different materials have different specific heats. Water has a high specific heat. It takes a lot of energy to raise the temperature of water. Silver has a low specific heat. It does not take much energy to raise the temperature of silver.

Answer the following question. Use your textbook and the ideas above.

9. Use the table to answer the question. If one kilogram of each of these materials absorbed the same amount of energy, which material would have the biggest change in temperature? _____

Specific Heat of Some Materials	
Material	**Specific Heat** (J/ kg·K)
Glass	837
Iron	450
Sand	800

Thermal Energy and Heat

The Transfer of Heat (pages 183–187)

How Is Heat Transferred? (pages 184–185)

Key Concept: **Heat is transferred by conduction, convection, and radiation.**

- There are three ways that heat can move: conduction, convection, and radiation.

- **Conduction** is heat moving from one particle to another. A metal spoon in hot soup gets warm because of conduction. Conduction happens between objects that are touching.

- **Convection** is heat transfer in a moving fluid. Gases and liquids are fluids. When a fluid is heated, it moves. The moving fluid transfers heat.

- **Radiation** is energy transfer by electromagnetic waves. The sun's energy travels to Earth by radiation. Matter is not needed for the transfer of energy by radiation.

Answer the following questions. Use your textbook and the ideas above.

1. Fill in the blanks in the table about heat transfer.

Heat Transfer	
Process	**How Heat Moves**
a. _____	in a moving fluid
b. _____	from one particle to another
c. _____	by electromagnetic waves

Thermal Energy and Heat

2. Which kind of heat transfer does not need matter?

    a. conduction

    b. convection

    c. radiation

3. Read each word in the box. In each sentence below, fill in one of the words.

    ┌───┐
    │ conduction   convection   radiation   │
    └───┘

    a. Energy moves in a pot of boiling water due to

    _____.

    b. The sun's energy travels to Earth by

    _____.

    c. A metal spoon gets warm in a bowl of hot soup

    due to _____.

Heat Moves One Way (page 186)

Key Concept: **If two objects have different temperatures, heat will flow from the warmer object to the colder one.**

• Heat can move in only one way. Heat always moves from a warmer object to a colder one.

• Heat will move between two objects until they are the same temperature.

Answer the following question. Use your textbook and the ideas above.

4. Read the words in the box. Use the words to fill in the blanks in the flowchart about heat.

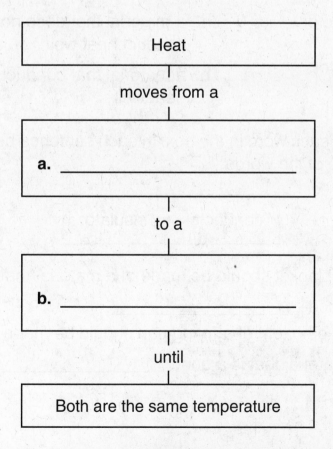

| Cooler object   Conduction   Warmer object |

Heat

moves from a

a. _____

to a

b. _____

until

Both are the same temperature

Name _____ Date _____ Class _____

Thermal Energy and Heat

Conductors and Insulators (pages 186–187)

Key Concept: **A conductor transfers thermal energy well. An insulator does not transfer thermal energy well.**

• A **conductor** is a material that transfers heat energy well. Metals are good conductors. A material that is a good conductor feels cool when you touch it. That is because a conductor easily transfers heat away from your body.

• An **insulator** is a material that does not conduct heat well. Wood and air are good insulators.

Answer the following questions. Use your textbook and the ideas above.

5. Draw a line from each term to its meaning.

Term	Meaning
conductor	**a.** a material that does not conduct heat well
insulator	**b.** a material that conducts heat well

6. Read each word in the box. In each sentence below, fill in one of the words.

> conductor   insulator

    a. A blanket should be made of a material that is a good _____.

    b. The bottom of a frying pan should be made of a material that is a good _____.

Thermal Energy and States of Matter (pages 190–194)

States of Matter (page 191)

Key Concept: **Most matter on Earth can exist in three states—solid, liquid, and gas.**

- Most matter on Earth is a solid, a liquid, or a gas. These three forms of matter are called **states**.

- The particles in a solid are packed together. They cannot move out of their places. That is why a solid does not change shape.

- The particles in a liquid are close together. They can move around, though. That is why a liquid can flow.

- The particles in a gas move very fast. They do not stay close together. That is why a gas spreads out and fills its container.

Answer the following questions. Use your textbook and the ideas above.

1. Read each word in the box. In each sentence below, fill in one of the words.

gas	solid	liquid

   a. The particles in a _____ do not change positions.

   b. The particles in a _____ move very quickly.

   c. The particles in a _____ are close together but can move around.

Thermal Energy and Heat

2. Read the words in the box. Use the words to label the
pictures.

solid   gas

Liquid

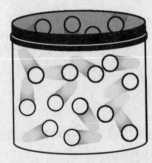

a. _____

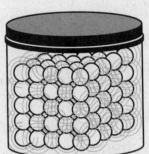

b. _____

Thermal Energy and Heat

Changes of State (pages 192–193)

Key Concept: **Matter can change from one state to another when thermal energy is absorbed or released.**

- A **change of state** is a change from one state of matter to another state of matter.

- A change from a solid to a liquid is called **melting**. An object absorbs thermal energy when it melts.

- A change from a liquid to a solid is called **freezing**. An object looses thermal energy when it freezes.

- A change from a liquid to a gas is called vaporization. During vaporization, a liquid absorbs thermal energy.

- When vaporization happens at the surface of a liquid, it is called **evaporation**. This is what causes puddles to dry up. At higher temperatures, vaporization can happen below the surface of the liquid. This is called **boiling**.

- A change from a gas to a liquid is called **condensation**. During condensation, a gas looses thermal energy.

Answer the following questions. Use your textbook and the ideas above.

3. A change from one state of matter to another state of matter is a(an) _____.

4. Draw a line from each term to its meaning.

Term	Meaning
freezing	**a.** a change from a liquid to a solid
melting	**b.** a change from a gas to a liquid
condensation	**c.** a change from a solid to a liquid

Thermal Energy and Heat

Thermal Expansion (page 194)

Key Concept: **As the thermal energy of matter increases, its particles spread out and the substance expands.**

- When an object is heated, it gets bigger. The particles in the object move apart from each other. This is called **thermal expansion**.

- When an object is cooled, it gets smaller. The particles in the object move closer together.

- A thermostat is a device that is used to turn heating systems on and off. A thermostat works because of thermal expansion.

Answer the following questions. Use your textbook and the ideas above.

5. When an object is heated and it gets bigger, it is called

   _____.

6. Circle the letter of each sentence that is true about thermal expansion.

   a. The particles in an object move apart when the object is heated.

   b. An object gets smaller as it gets warmer.

   c. A thermostat works because of thermal expansion.

Thermal Energy and Heat

Uses of Heat (pages 195–199)

Heat Engines (pages 195–197)

Key Concept: **Heat engines transform thermal energy to mechanical energy.**

• A **heat engine** changes thermal energy to mechanical energy. There are two kinds of heat engines: external combustion engines and internal combustion engines.

• **External combustion engines** burn fuel outside the engine. A steam engine is an example.

• **Internal combustion engines** burn fuel inside the engine. Cars and trucks use internal combustion engines.

Answer the following questions. Use your textbook and the ideas above.

1. Draw a line from each term to its meaning.

Term	Meaning
internal combustion engine	**a.** an engine that burns fuel inside of the engine
heat engine	**b.** an engine that burns fuel outside of the engine
external combustion engine	**c.** any engine that changes thermal energy to mechanical energy

2. Read each word in the box. In each sentence below, fill in one of the words.

| car engine   steam engine |

a. An example of an external combustion engine is

a _____.

b. An example of an internal combustion engine is

a _____.

Cooling Systems (pages 198–199)

Key Concept: **A refrigerator is a device that transfers thermal energy from inside the refrigerator to the room outside.**

- A cooling system transfers heat to keep things cool.

- A refrigerator is one kind of cooling system. A **refrigerant** is a material used in a refrigerator. A refrigerant absorbs and releases heat.

- An air conditioner is another kind of cooling system. Air conditioners are used to keep buildings and cars cool.

Answer the following questions. Use your textbook and the ideas above.

3. Circle the letter of each sentence that is true about cooling systems.
   a. Cooling systems transfer heat.
   b. A car engine is an example of a cooling system.
   c. Cooling systems use refrigerants to transfer heat.

Thermal Energy and Heat

4. Read the words in the box. Use the words to fill in the
blanks in the flowchart about cooling systems.

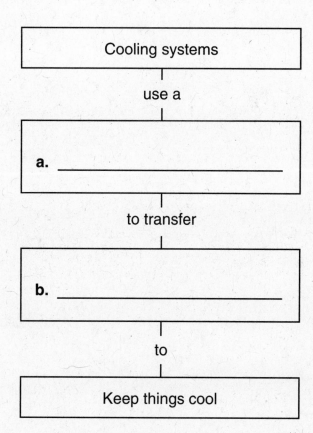

| Heat   Refrigerator   Refrigerant |

Cooling systems

use a

a. _____

to transfer

b. _____

to

Keep things cool